FULL CIRCLE MARKETING

Transform Your Marketing and Turn Customers Into Evangelists

WAYNE MULLINS

Full Circle Marketing
Copyright © 2021 by Wayne Mullins
Published by Ugly Mug Marketing

Bulk orders: books@uglymugmarketing.com

Print ISBN: 978-0-578-97651-8
Ebook ISBN: 978-0-578-97652-5

UglyMugMarketing.com

To Heather, Truett,
Jett, Hudson and Harper,
don't settle.

It's not going to be easy,
but it's going to be worth it.

CONTENTS

INTRODUCTION

*P*eople assume marketing has to be expensive, complex, and complicated.

They're wrong!

Marketing can be simple, effective, and affordable. But the only way to make your marketing simple, effective, and affordable is to be strategic. In an ever-changing, ever-evolving world, being strategic isn't easy. The lure of the *latest and greatest* marketing tool or app is enough to persuade even the most skeptical among us to ditch our strategy and chase the *new*. And if the tools and apps aren't enough to tempt us, we have plenty of self-proclaimed gurus pitching the marketing hack they discovered, all from their garage with a rented Lamborghini in the background. (Looking at you Tai Lopez.) With all the noise, how could you not believe marketing is expensive, complex, and complicated?

This belief that marketing has to be expensive, complex, and complicated is a myth. A narrative that we are being sold, and as much as I wish it weren't true, it's a myth we've bought hook, line, and sinker. I'm reminded of the wise words Steven Pressfield shared in his book *The War of Art*:

> Do you regularly ingest any substance, controlled or otherwise, whose aim is the alleviation of depression, anxiety, etc.? I offer the following experience: I once worked as a writer for a big New York ad agency. Our boss used to tell us: "Invent a disease. Come up with the disease," he said, "and we can sell the cure." Attention Deficit Disorder, Seasonal Affect Disorder, Social Anxiety Disorder. These aren't diseases, they're marketing ploys. Doctors didn't discover them, copywriters did. Marketing departments did. Drug companies did.

This isn't the book to debate the accuracy of Mr. Pressfield's comment, but it is the book to help you shift your marketing narrative. During our time together, my job is to show you a process that can make your marketing both simple and effective. Notice I didn't say simple *or* effective. I said *simple and effective.* Both are attainable with the right strategy. Both are possible when you choose to let go of the false narrative you've bought that effective marketing is complicated and unpredictable.

Over the next pages you're going to discover two fundamental marketing strategies. Marketing strategies that work every single time they are used, and in many ways, these two fundamental strategies are like natural laws. And just like natural laws, you can choose to ignore them, or even pretend they don't exist, but your decision doesn't invalidate the laws. Jump out of an airplane, and you don't invalidate the law of gravity; you prove it. The same is true for the strategies you'll discover in the pages of this book. You can ignore them, or even intentionally violate them, but your decision won't invalidate their reality. Instead your results, or lack thereof, will merely confirm their existence.

You may be thinking, *that's a bold claim to make in the first few words of this book*. I agree, so let me briefly explain why I place so much confidence in these strategies. To begin, I've not only witnessed the results of these strategies in my own company, but also for hundreds of other organizations that have applied them. The next reason for my bold claim is simply this: these marketing strategies aren't based on a tool, tactic, app, or what some "guru" shared with me in secret. Instead, they are based on the core fundamentals of human nature. This is not to say that human nature does not shift or change over time, because it does, but that changes are very slow and progressive. Therein lies the power of these marketing strategies—human nature. If your marketing strategies are in alignment with the way human nature works, you'll succeed.

A brief warning before we get started. On the surface these strategies may seem too simple or even *too good to be true*. If you aren't careful, their simplicity may tempt you to dismiss them, and that would be a mistake. As marketers, we are prone to complexity bias. Complexity bias is a logical fallacy that leads us to give undue credence to complex concepts. We mistakenly believe simple solutions can not, or will not, be effective. So if you are going to get the most from our time together, let go of your complexity bias. You have my permission.

Let's begin!

PART I

THERE ARE NO SECRETS

CHAPTER 1

MEET THE MARKETING ROCK

*T*his rock has generated over a million dollars in revenue for our company!

Nope, that's not a typo.

And nope, that's not an exaggeration.

In fact, $1million dollars in revenue is an extremely conservative figure.

I'll give you the specifics in just a minute, but for now, let me explain what makes this rock so magical.

Are you ready for this?

Okay, here it is: Nothing!

That's right, nothing!

It's nothing more than a smooth rock, just like one you'd pick up on the side of the road as a kid, with words written on it with a permanent marker.

The words themselves aren't particularly magical either. They simply say:

"Effective Marketing Doesn't Have To Be Expensive.
www.uglymugmarketing.com"

I agree with you—not overly impressive nor magical. So where does the magic come from?

All of its magic comes from two ancient, mostly forgotten marketing formulas. One of these marketing formulas was originally tested, used, and written about more than one hundred years ago, in 1910.

Oh, how the world has changed since 1910. Think about it, cars and electricity were rarities, news was only consumed via print media, and the majority of people never traveled more than twenty miles from where they were born. The world seemed to move at a much slower pace back then.

Despite how much the world has changed, the triggers that influence human behavior have remained relatively unchanged.

I know, I know. That is counterintuitive to what we naturally believe. Somehow we seem to think human psychology and persuasion have *changed with the times*. They haven't! Despite what the Gary Vaynerchuks of the world want you to believe, what works today is based on the exact same fundamentals that worked in 1910. All of the *poster-child* social media gurus (Gary Vaynerchuk, Grant Cardone, Amy Porterfield, etc.) want you to believe people make decisions differently than they did in the past.

Of course the gurus want you to think this way. After all, their most recent book, course, or event contains the exact formula that's working *right now*. Each of these *poster-child* gurus will gladly share *what's working now* in exchange for a few (or many) of your dollars. Do you know what's beautiful about what they preach? As the world changes, it gives them the ability to sell you the newest version of *what's working now.*

Look, you're welcome to join the *poster-child* guru of the month club if you'd like. But my prediction is that you end up frustrated with your results, and with a few less dollars in your pocket.

The beauty of the formulas you're about to discover is you don't have to change them every time a new social media platform is launched, or every time a *poster-child* tells you they've discovered a new magic marketing formula. Okay, so help me down off my soapbox so I can continue sharing with you the story of the marketing rock.

HOW DID IT WORK?

In 2010, I was broke. My marketing company was failing. Not for lack of trying. I was eagerly soaking up every word that dribbled from *poster-child* entrepreneurs. I'd spend hours watching videos, reading books, and attempting to implement what I'd learned. And yet, nothing seemed to work. I was busy stacking up failures, while time and my cash reserves were running out. Not sure if you can relate to that, but if not, lemme just say, it wasn't fun!

Most of my days were spent trying to convince business owners they needed to give up on brand building and transition to direct response marketing.

Brand building is what the majority of businesses do, not because of how well it works, but merely because it's easy. It's easy to say, "come shop with us; we've been in business 20 years, have great customer service, and are awesome people." Nothing wrong with that approach, but brand building marketing has three specific weaknesses:

- Everyone can make similar claims. When you use general platitudes, so can all your competitors.
- You don't know if it's working. When your company name and a list of platitudes is your marketing message, how do you know which of your marketing campaigns is working?
- It's lazy. Brand building campaigns don't force you to think through the Natural Progression. (More on the Natural Progression a bit later.)

Direct Response Marketing, in many ways, is the polar opposite of brand building. At its core, Direct Response Marketing (DRM) is about accountability, holding each campaign and each ad accountable for the results they produce. What makes DRM unique is each ad has a specific (trackable) call to action, giving you the ability to know which ads/campaigns are working, and which aren't.

Finally after hearing my one millionth "no," (okay, maybe it wasn't that many rejections, but it sure felt that way), burning through all my savings, and piling up a massive amount of debt, I grudgingly decided it was time to try a different approach.

So instead of continually beating my head against the wall trying to convince people to give DRM a try, I decided to create a tool that would show them the power—and the marketing rock was born.

The process was:

1. Go to the garden center and buy a few smooth rocks
2. Write on them with a Sharpie
3. Leave them around town

Simple, right?!

At this point you're probably wondering, *that's simple and makes sense, but how did it generate so much revenue?* During the rest of our time together, I'm going to walk through the entire process in detail. You are going to discover the psychology behind why it works and how you can create your own marketing system that consistently delivers results. Let's begin with why it works.

CHAPTER 2

THERE IS NO HOPE

In the last chapter, we talked about the functional part of how the marketing rock worked. In this chapter, we're going to talk about why it worked. But before we look into all the reasons why it worked, we need to ensure we're on the same page about what marketing is, and what marketing isn't.

After asking thousands of entrepreneurs to define marketing, it has become clear that most people use the term marketing and advertising interchangeably. And that is a mistake, because they aren't the same. You see, advertising is merely one small component of marketing. If all you're doing is advertising it's tough to get the results you want. You can't be great at marketing, if you don't know what it is.

WHAT MARKETING IS

A Google search will quickly reveal dozens of definitions of marketing. All are good, some are valid, but reviewing them will leave you confused. Which definition is right? Which is wrong? Instead of spending your time and energy trying to figure out which definition you like best, let's follow our friend Simon Sinek's advice and start with *why*. Once we get clear about all of our *whys,* it automatically creates clarity around the *what*. Here are a few marketing related *whys* you may be struggling with:

- Why does marketing have to be so complicated?
- Why does marketing have to be so expensive?
- Why should I devote my time and energy to marketing?
- Why does marketing even matter to my organization?
- Why do most of my marketing efforts end in failure?

What other *whys* do you struggle with when it comes to your marketing? I strongly encourage you to pause, put down this book, and spend a few minutes listing and examining your *whys*. Go ahead, I'll be here when you get back.

If you're reading these words, I'm assuming you've defined your whys, so let's move on.

For something to make an impact, it must be understood. The best way for something to be understood is to keep it simple. As Donald Miller says, "if you confuse, you lose." So when it comes to defining marketing, I believe in keeping it simple. The simplest definition of marketing I've been able to come up with is this:

Marketing is your ability to attract and keep a customer.
Simple, right? Simple, but not easy.

Marketing is more holistic than merely attracting new customers. It should encompass every aspect required to both attract and keep your customers coming back for more.

Before we get into the specifics of attracting and keeping, we must first talk about...

WHAT MARKETING ISN'T

Marketing shouldn't be mystical. Your marketing and the results it produces must be more corollary (X input equals Y result). Getting results from your marketing must be more than happenstance. Marketing isn't about a hope and a prayer. Your marketing shouldn't be dependent on which media rep has the biggest promotion this month. Do any of those describe your marketing? This isn't the time for excuses or giving yourself an easy pass. This is the time to look yourself squarely in the mirror and face the truth. Here's a harsh truth…

Your marketing system is perfectly designed for the results you're getting.

Hope is NOT a marketing strategy.

If you're not getting the results you'd like, it's a waste of time to sit around and complain. Instead, let's focus on remaking the system that is producing these unacceptable marketing results. You may be thinking, *but I don't really have a marketing system*. You do have a marketing system. The question is, were you intentional in its creation? Your results, or lack thereof, are the best indication of the effectiveness of your marketing system. And to be clear, hope is not a marketing strategy!

As we've already discussed, marketing is simply your ability to attract and keep a customer. Both are equally important. But both take place in different realms. The first (attracting), takes place in the realm where the money is still in your prospect's pocket. The attracting component of your marketing should be designed to bring people up to the point of sale, at which point it becomes your sales or customer service department's role to complete the transaction.

If you're like most entrepreneurs I've worked with, you tend to spend most of your time on the *attracting* part of marketing. But believe it or not, the *Keeping a Customer* portion of your marketing is where you should be devoting more of your time and attention. We'll spend more time talking in depth about Keeping a Customer in Chapters 7 & 8, but for now, here are a few critical factors you need to know about *Keeping a Customer*. Keeping a Customer is:

- a long-term strategy, with an infinitely higher ROI than the *attracting* side
- the closest thing to building a perpetual motion marketing machine—by creating evangelists for your business
- an immediate differentiator for your business
- a powerful way to keep the main thing, *the main thing*— relationships with your customers

How well are you doing at keeping customers? How serious are you about converting your customers into evangelists? Hang on, before you answer, here's a litmus test. Pull out your financials. Go to your marketing/advertising expenses. Now how much of your marketing budget is allocated to *attracting* customers, and how much is allocated to *keeping* customers?

No, I'm not going to tell you that by having a great product or service you will keep customers. My assumption is that

YOUR MARKETING SYSTEM is perfectly designed for the **RESULTS YOU'RE GETTING.**

your product or service is already phenomenal. You see, there is far more involved in keeping customers than having an amazing product, although that goes a long way. A bit later I'm going to show you how to retain customers in such a way that they can't help but tell others about you.

I've asked that same question to thousands of entrepreneurs, and the results are always the same. Over 95% of their marketing budgets are allocated for the attracting of new customers, with 5% or less set aside for nurturing relationships with existing customers. Take just a few minutes and evaluate your marketing budget to see where your allocations fall.

Think for a minute about the brands you love most. Although your favorite brands may be in several different industries and provide different products, I'd be willing to bet you have a relationship with them. What I mean is that you feel, at least on some level, that they care more about you than merely taking your money. You feel they value you more than a mere transaction. The brands with the deepest connection with their customers win in the long run.

The difference between a transactional and a relational company rests in how they value their customer relationships. If you are after long-term success, then your customers must receive more value than they give in exchange. It's your responsibility as a marketer to ensure your products or services are of more value than they cost your customers, and that what you offer consistently exceeds expectations. Do these two things (provide value and exceed expectations) with enough consistency and for long enough, and success will be inevitable. Notice I didn't say "*easy*" and I didn't say "*quick.*" If you want long-term success, you must use long-term thinking and implement long-term strategies.

Now that we've taken a brief detour down the *keeping* side of marketing, let's return to the *attracting* side and how to create your own marketing rock. To begin, I'd like to introduce you to my often forgotten friend, AIDA.

CHAPTER 3

FOLLOWING AIDA

*T*here's value in the invisible.

Value in keeping secret formulas secret.

The recipe for Coca Cola is locked away in a carefully guarded vault. There's immense value in their secret recipe. The value lies not in the recipe itself, but in what the recipe creates—the drink. Coca Cola makes its money selling the drink, not selling the recipe.

The marketing world works differently, particularly when it comes to marketing gurus. Gurus don't make their money selling a product, but instead by selling the recipe over and over again. And once their audience's taste has changed, the gurus always seem to magically discover a new recipe they can package and sell. Their recipe changes to follow the money.

In this chapter, I'm going to give you a recipe. A recipe the value of which is not found in its secrecy—it's been around for more than one hundred years—but in the customers and evangelists it produces. Let me introduce you to AIDA.

AIDA is a recipe. In many ways AIDA has become a secret recipe, not because it has been carefully hidden, but because we, as marketers, forgot about it in our pursuit of the latest tactic or marketing hack.

You see, AIDA was originally tested, used, and written about way back in 1910. Here we are more than a century later, and the formula is still as relevant as when it was first tested and shared with the world.

AIDA is more than a recipe, more than a tactic. It's a framework. You can put virtually any marketing strategy or tactic onto the AIDA framework, and achieve better results.

Impatience is what gets most marketers into trouble. It's natural for us to want prospects to pull out their wallets as quickly as possible. But if we are going to be strategic, we must learn to temper our need for speed. In our impatience, we often completely ignore some fundamental human psychology. The effects of ignoring this basic psychology may not show up immediately, but they always show up in our results.

Following AIDA helps hold even the most impatient among us accountable to a few fundamentals of human psychology. AIDA is an acronym, and its power lies in what each letter represents.

ATTENTION

Where attention goes, money flows!

You can have the best product in the world, but if no one knows about it, no one will buy it. You can create the most amazing ads in the world, but if you never publish them, no one will buy. In order for people to purchase your product, they must first know about it. In order for people to know about it, they must first learn about it. And in order for people to learn about your product, they must first be aware of your messaging. This awareness can only happen once you capture their attention.

You already know this, but attention is a precious commodity. Research shows the average American is exposed to more than 5,000 marketing messages per day. That's a lot of competition for your audience's attention. And to make matters worse, the rate of content generated has grown exponentially in recent decades. The amount of new content created each day in 2020 was 2.5 quintillion data bytes.[1] Insane! And the average adult now consumes more than 7.5 hours of media each day![2]

With so much noise and distraction vying for the attention of your prospective customers, you have no choice but to be strategic if you want a chance at success. Unless you have a lot of extra time, and money to waste, you can't afford to try a bunch of things and see what works. To succeed you need to reduce the amount of time and money it takes for your marketing to produce a positive ROI.

Capturing attention doesn't have to be complex or complicated. No need to run an ad on the Super Bowl. No need for massive marketing budgets. There are countless methods you could use to grab attention, but all have one thing in common. They interrupt a pattern (this is known as a pattern interrupt) that is taking place in the minds of their prospective customers.

1   https://www.statista.com/topics/1536/media-use
2   https://www.takeo.ai/can-you-guess-how-much-data-is-generated-every-day

Pattern interrupts come from the world of Neuro Linguistic Programming (NLP). We don't have the time or space here, but the simplest way to explain NLP is using the analogy of a vinyl record. Vinyl records are created by cutting grooves into the vinyl. The needle on the record player then sits inside the groove as the record goes round and round.

The same happens in our lives. The majority of our lives are spent inside grooves we've created over time. Those grooves are our habits and beliefs. Research shows that as much as 40 percent of our days are run according to our subconscious habits. It's these subconscious habits that keep us sane. If we had to think about every single thing we do each day, we'd go crazy. Let's take walking for example. Imagine having to think about every single component required to walk.

These subconscious sequences control almost every area of our lives, as well as your prospects' lives. So if we are to have any hope of capturing their attention, we must break the patterns of these automated sequences. We must stand out from all the other noise and distractions vying for their attention.

A few ideas for breaking someone's pattern:

- Do something unexpected
- Show up in an unexpected place
- Show up in an unexpected way
- Show up through an unexpected path

Our marketing rock checks all of those boxes. Let's explore how. For starters, most people

People are interested in their interests, not your products or services.

don't expect to see a rock with something written on it (that's unexpected). We would place these marketing rocks in places that people wouldn't expect to find them. We would leave them on tables in restaurants and coffee shops, in grocery stores and hotel lobbies. When you sit down at a restaurant for dinner, or are browsing the supermarket, you don't expect to see a rock with a message on it.

When you see a rock in these unexpected places, you can't help but give it your attention. However, as we'll soon discover, getting attention is just the beginning. Getting attention without the next step in AIDA is wasted energy and effort. Before we move on to the next step, here are a few questions to help you find ways to capture attention.

- What are your competitors doing to capture attention?
- What would be the opposite of what they're doing?
- What are some unexpected places you could show up?
- What connections could you leverage that would provide additional opportunities for capturing attention?
- How could you leverage or incentivize existing customers to help capture additional attention?

Taking the time to answer those questions will help ensure you fully capture potential customers' attention so that you can then pique their interest.

INTEREST

People are interested in their interests, not your products or services.

If we want to leverage the attention we've captured, we must pique, and keep, our prospects' interest. To be successful with this step, you must have a thorough understanding of your audience. It's impossible to pique their interest if you don't know what they are interested in being, doing, having, or avoiding. This requires more than surface level knowledge. You must understand their problems and their desires. Getting to this level of "knowing" them is more than a five minute process, and it's certainly more than merely assuming we *know* our customers.

Over the years, two exercises have proven extremely valuable in helping our clients get to know their customers and potential customers on a deeper level. The first is to create a customer avatar. You can download our Customer Avatar Worksheet at www.yourfullcirclemarketing.com/bonus. It's a great starting point, but it should only be the beginning. Completing this worksheet will help you identify attributes and surface-level emotions, but your work doesn't end there. Let's walk through a few questions.

If you know your ideal customer drives a pickup truck, this information now provides you with a bit more context for helping understand their interest, even if you don't sell vehicles. What clues could driving a truck provide? What if your ideal customer drives a sports car? What clues may this give you about your prospective customer?

What is their family situation? Are they married? Have kids? How many? While it's easy to assume answers to these questions won't have any influence on your ability to ignite their interest, that assumption is wrong. The more you understand your target audience, the more effective you'll be, not just at getting their attention , but in marketing as a whole. If you're going to be successful in marketing, what is of interest to your prospective customers must become of interest to you.

Let's circle back to our marketing rock for a minute. If you boil businesses down to their basics, there are only two types of problems that exist: 1) fulfillment problems 2) marketing problems. Every problem a business could possibly face can fit under one of those two categories. Now imagine you're a business owner sitting down at your favorite restaurant, and you happen to find one of our marketing rocks sitting on your table. The rock would capture your attention, and the words (Effective Marketing Doesn't Have to Be Expensive) would intrigue you.

Even if you were in the midst of an important lunch meeting, the words we used on the marketing rock might make you question the effectiveness of your marketing. *Are the TV spots we just purchased effective? What about the money we're spending on radio? How do I know if my marketing is actually effective?* As these questions ruminate through your mind, the marketing rock has piqued your interest and is building the desire for more effective marketing. With those first two parts of AIDA accomplished, let's look at the "D."

DESIRE

*Desire starts with the knowledge
that something better is possible.*

Interest turns to desire when we begin to realize that another—*better*—option is available to us. We may be interested in a variety of things, but we don't desire them if we don't believe there is a chance of obtaining them.

As marketers, if we're able to evoke desire in the hearts and minds of our prospects, our work becomes infinitely easier.

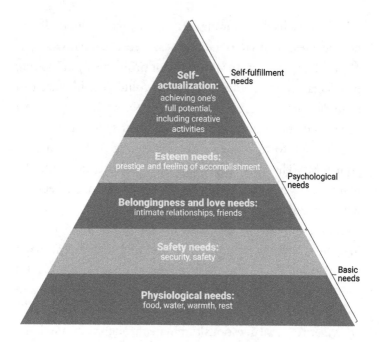

When people truly desire something, they begin selling themselves on why they need it. Once they desire it, our job simply becomes removing the obstacles that may be standing in their way. We'll talk about removing obstacles in Chapter 9, but for now let's talk about evoking, or better yet, stoking desire.

We don't have the time or space here to do a deep dive into psychology, but there are certain fundamental things all humans need. And until we understand our prospects' needs, we can't begin stoking their desires. *Maslow's Hierarchy of Needs* is a great place to start exploring the needs and desires of your prospective customers.

Where does your product or service fit? Does it fulfill basic needs, psychological needs, self-fulfilling needs, or some combination of each? Using the needs pyramid, take a minute to identify which need(s) your product fulfills.

To help illustrate what the process may look like, let's imagine your product is delicious, organic, vegan protein bars. What need(s) would your product fulfill? On the surface your product meets *basic needs*—as food. But if we examine it in more depth, we'll see your product fulfills several needs in the pyramid. Let's run through each.

Because your product is organic, your customers consider it safer than non-organic products, thus checking off the *safety needs* box. Thanks in part to your bars being vegan, they reinforce the sense of *belonging* your customers feel. After all, they are part of a group (vegans) who believe it is better for animals, our environment, and their bodies, to not consume foods derived from animals. And whether they'd admit it or not, your product also fulfills their *esteem needs*. In a small way, your premium priced bars make purchasers feel a sense of prestige. Maybe the prestige comes from the high price, compared to other bars, or from the fact they know they are part of a small group who cares enough about animals, the environment, and their health.

So what about your product or service? Which need(s) does it fulfill? Take a few minutes to examine your product or service through Maslow's Needs Pyramid.

Now with those answers in hand, let's talk about your customers' desires. As we talked about earlier, desire begins with the knowledge that something better may be possible. Often, though not always, we know something better is available because we see others enjoying the benefits of that better thing.

Think about the iPhone. When it was released in 2007, the cell phone world was ruled by Blackberries and their tiny keypads. Apple brilliantly promoted their phone as something more. It wasn't about a better keypad, as it didn't have one. All of their marketing centered around possibility. Put down this book for a second, do a quick Google search of the original iPhone commercials, and watch a few of them.

The core of their commercials' messaging was: there is something better available, something that gives you possibilities. We have it. It's the iPhone. That's it. Simple, and yet extremely profound. They didn't need to compare the iPhone to competitors. They didn't have to show a long list of features or benefits. Instead, they did what Apple does best. They evoked our desire for something better. Even if your product isn't as cool or cutting edge as an Apple product, with strategic planning you can position and promote it in such a way that sparks desire.

So how exactly did our marketing rock evoke desire? Our avatar, a busy entrepreneur, has a strong desire for results and growth. He understands marketing is one of the key fulcrum points they must control if they are to reach their desires. After decades of being an entrepreneur and working directly with thousands of them, experience has shown me that the majority of business owners assume marketing is expensive and ineffective. So the simple statement we wrote on the marketing rock, *"Effective marketing doesn't have to be expensive,"* speaks to their desire for effective and affordable marketing and their hope that marketing will deliver both results and growth.

This language sparks business owners' interest and evokes their desire for something better. And your marketing message must do the exact same thing. Now for the last step of AIDA. It does no good to capture their attention, pique their interest, and evoke their desire, if you don't call them to action. You have to give them a way to satisfy their desire.

ACTION

A clear singular path for exactly what to do next.

"Nothing happens," as Zig Ziglar used to say, "until somebody sells something." And in that same vein, nothing happens with your marketing rock unless someone takes action. If you capture attention, but don't pique interest, you've wasted that attention. Ignite interest, but don't spark desire, and your message falls flat. And eliciting desire without providing a specific call to action means you've done nothing more than waste time. You will have wasted your time, but more importantly, you will have wasted your prospective customers' time.

The goal of your marketing should be to make selling unnecessary. This means by the time they've finished progressing through your marketing funnel, people don't need someone from your team to try and convince them to purchase. Effective marketing does the selling. For that to happen, you must include a call to action in your marketing message. Don't ask, "Should I include a call to action?", but instead, "What will my call to action be?" But before you can determine your call to action, there are four factors you must consider:

1. What is the next logical step I need them to take?

Think about the big picture and how you can use your marketing to lead people through your sales funnel. This will guide you as to what the next step should be. This could be placing a phone call, scheduling a consultation, making a purchase, or taking any other step that leads them closer to pulling out their wallet.

2. How will they complete this step?

To ensure you are using the right call to action, you must think through how they will take the action you want them to take. Will they visit a web page, make a phone call, or visit your store?

3. What burdens or obstacles may be in their path?

Now that you know the next step and have thought through how they will complete it, you've got to work to remove any burdens or obstacles that may arise once they act on their desire and follow through on your call to action.

4. Will their action be enough?

The best marketing pieces move people closer to a purchasing decision. Depending on the marketing piece you are creating, the action you are requesting they take may not be enough for them to make a purchase decision, and that's okay. It's okay if the goal of your marketing piece is to get a phone call. But it's not okay if you don't know what the next steps, after the phone rings, will be. It's okay if the goal of your piece is to get them to visit your website. But it's not okay if you don't have a plan in place to ensure that at some point, that initial website visit turns into a sale.

Too often we, as marketers, expect too much from our campaigns. When we expect too much from individual campaigns, we are setting ourselves up for frustration and campaign failure. It's important to remember that each campaign should be designed to bring people one step closer to a purchasing decision. That's it! One step. Stop being so demanding of your campaigns, and instead start thinking through what additional campaigns you will need to ensure people move one step closer.

The reality is their action from your marketing will not likely lead to a sale, and that's okay. We must simply devote some time to discovering what we need to do to illuminate the next step they need to take. This, whatever *this* is, becomes our next campaign. We'll explore this in much more detail when we talk about the Natural Progression.

AIDA HAS A PROBLEM

With a bit of practice and intention, AIDA has the power to transform every aspect of your marketing. But AIDA has a problem. The problem isn't with its effectiveness, nor its complexity. Actually, the opposite is what causes the issues. AIDA's problem is that it is too simple. You see, if we aren't

The

BEST

MARKETING

PIECES

move people

closer to a

PURCHASING

DECISION.

careful, its simplicity will deceive us. Our natural inclination is to doubt that simple things can be effective. As mentioned in the introduction, this is known as complexity bias. The more complex a solution, the more inherent value we believe it has. And if we're not careful, that belief will cause us to marginalize AIDA.

The beauty of AIDA is that it can be applied to any marketing campaign regardless of the platform, regardless of the goal. But even as wonderful as AIDA is at helping us craft marketing messages that inspire action, it doesn't provide a framework for how we should approach our entire marketing system. And if your goal is to make your marketing both simple and effective, you'll need a framework to build your marketing on, and that's where the Natural Progression comes into play.

PART II

THE FIRST HALF

CHAPTER 4

GOING NATURAL

*H*ave you ever stepped back and thought about how people flow through a business? You know, like how do people transition from being a prospect to a customer? Maybe your business is different, but last time I checked, people don't just magically show up at our doorstep and hand us money. There are specific steps prospects go through when making buying decisions, a natural path they all follow. This path is the same regardless of what you sell. The only variance is the amount of time they spend at each phase.

Until you understand how your prospects traverse this path, your marketing is based on nothing more than a hope and a prayer. You waste your time grabbing the *latest and greatest* marketing tool only to then hope and pray it works. How's that working for you? Intuitively, you know there has to be a better way, something more predictable, something more strategic. Fortunately, there is a predictable and strategic way, and it's called the Natural Progression.

In many ways, the Natural Progression is like gravity. It works every single time whether we acknowledge it or not. When it comes to making purchasing decisions, there are specific stages that people go through every single time. Every customer who has ever purchased your product or service has gone through the exact same stages.

The beauty of the Natural Progression is that once you understand it, you can intentionally influence customers at each of the stages. With a bit of strategy, you can help influence people to move more quickly through the stages, and turn your existing customers into "evangelists" for your company, your products, and your mission. Imagine how transformational that would be for your business. The reality is, once you understand the Natural Progression, you'll possess the power to accomplish all of the above. Your marketing will no longer live in the land of hopes and prayers, but instead in the world of strategy and intention.

So what is this seemingly magical thing called the Natural Progression? Let's take a look.

Over the next few chapters, we're going to take a look at each of the stages of the Natural Progression in detail. But for now, let me give you a brief overview of each stage.

STRANGERS

Who are these people? We define a Stranger as anyone who doesn't know about your company or products, but that you believe would benefit from the value your product or service provides. The second part of that sentence is an important distinction. A stranger isn't merely anyone who doesn't know

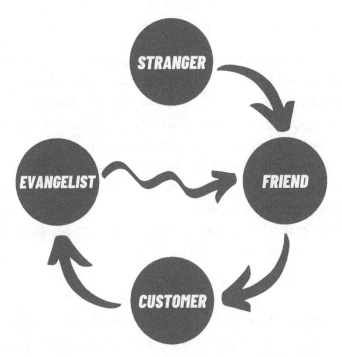

about you, but specifically someone who would benefit from your product or service. One way to think of strangers is as people who would be great customers if they only knew about you.

FRIENDS

The primary difference between a Stranger and a Friend is that friends both know about, and *like*, your company and/ or the products/services you provide. Think about it. It would be tough for a vegan to be a friend of yours if you sell grass-fed beef. Don't lose sleep over this. Instead, devote your attention to making friends out of people who would naturally be inclined to derive value from what you sell.

CUSTOMERS

A Customer is someone who has handed you money in exchange for whatever it is you sell. That part is obvious. But what isn't always obvious are the steps that person took to move from a Friend to Customer. The biggest factor required for someone to make the journey from a Friend to a Customer is trust. Before folks are going to pull out their wallets, they have to trust that your product or service is going to do what you say it's going to do. They have to trust that what you're selling is more valuable than the money they are paying for it.

EVANGELISTS

Without a doubt, this is the most overlooked aspect of the Natural Progression. And yet, creating evangelists is the most high-leverage marketing activity you can do. Evangelists are those who go out and tell others about how great your product or service is. When properly trained, they will become your most effective sales force.

The beauty of the Natural Progression is that it shows us the exact campaign we should be running. It removes so much of the guesswork that surrounds marketing. We get in trouble, become overwhelmed, and end up with ineffective marketing when we demand too much from one campaign. Through the lens of the Natural Progression, we can see that we'll need at least three campaigns: one to convert strangers into friends, another to turn friends into customers, and a final campaign designed to convert customers into evangelists.

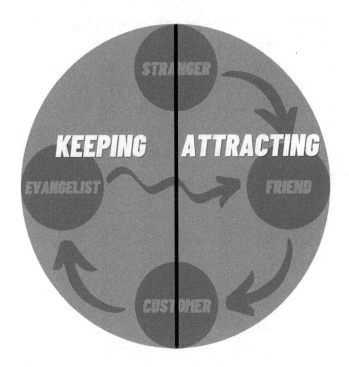

Over the next few chapters, we'll dive into more depth about each of the stages of the Natural Progression and talk through what you should specifically focus on. But before we move on, there's one more way I want you to think about the Natural Progression.

Back in Chapter 2, you'll remember, we defined marketing as your ability to both attract and keep a customer. If we aren't careful, we can easily fall into the trap of believing that once we've attracted the customer, and they have purchased our product, our work is done. But as the Natural Progression reveals, we still have a bit more work to do after making the sell. As the Natural Progression above shows, everything on the right side is about attracting, and the left side is about keeping.

This is significant because when you're strategic about your marketing, you'll devote time and budget to both attracting and keeping. If you aren't sure exactly what that could look like for you, don't worry; we will walk through it step by step over the next chapters. But for now, let's look at strangers in more detail.

CHAPTER 5

STRANGER THINGS

The first step to strategic marketing is learning to properly identify Strangers. A Stranger is anyone who doesn't know about your company or products/services, and who you believe could benefit from the value your product or service provides. In order for your marketing to be both efficient and effective, you can't waste money reaching people who will never be interested in what you sell. Sounds obvious, and yet the majority of entrepreneurs are sloppy with where and how their marketing dollars are invested. Most throw huge portions of their marketing budgets at campaigns that reach people who will never be interested in what they sell. If your marketing is going to be efficient and effective, it has to be strategic. Strategic marketing is about holding each dollar accountable for a specific result, and that accountability begins with who you define as Strangers.

When it comes to identifying Strangers, the most strategic place you can begin is with the customer avatar you created back in Chapter 3. (You did create your customer avatar, didn't you?! If not, I'll wait here for you to stop and finish it.) Without a clearly defined customer avatar, every human being on planet earth is a Stranger you'll need to reach with your marketing. Not sure how big your annual marketing budget is, but if it isn't in the hundreds of millions of dollars, it would probably be best to narrow the number of Strangers you will need to reach through your marketing. Having your Avatar clearly defined allows you to drastically narrow the number of people you need your marketing messages to reach.

Thanks to your avatar, you should now have a specific audience of Strangers you are going to market to, so now let's clarify the goal of your initial marketing campaign.

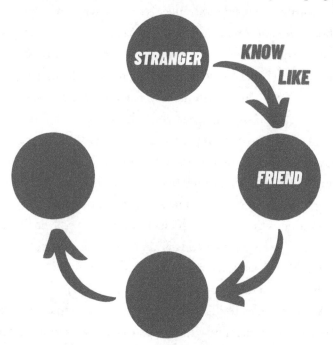

The goal for this particular campaign is simply to convert Strangers into Friends. Nothing more. Nothing less. As we discussed in the previous chapter, the two core components needed to make this journey (from Stranger to Customer) are *knowing* and *liking*. Let's walk through an example of how this may look.

Think about your own personal life. Do you consider people you don't know to be your personal friends? Probably not. Do you consider people who don't like you to be your close personal friends? Sure, you may be cordial with them, but you probably don't consider these people to be your close personal friends. The same applies to your business. People can't be Friends of your business if they don't know you exist. And to take it one step further, people who know about your business, but don't like the products you provide, will likely never be your Friends. Converting Strangers to Friends is the first step required of all effective marketing. Let's look at an example of how this may happen.

MEET HEATHER

Heather decides she needs a new website for her business. She sits down at her computer and types "website design company" into her search engine. Ugly Mug Marketing is listed in her results. So she thinks to herself, *that's a stupid name*, but clicks the link anyway.

At this point she's a Stranger. At Ugly Mug Marketing, we don't know she's out there, but she's still a prospect because she is looking for a website design company and could benefit from our web design services. After spending a few minutes learning more about what we do, viewing our portfolio, and reading through the dozens of testimonials, she feels we *may* be a good choice. While reviewing our portfolio, Heather sees that we built a website for a restaurant owned by her cousin's wife and decides to give her a call to ask if she enjoyed working with us.

Great news! Her cousin's wife had great things to say about working with us. At this point, even though we (at Ugly Mug Marketing) still don't know Heather exists, she now *knows* about us and *likes* us because of the positive things she was told about us. Even though we have never talked to Heather, she has moved from a Stranger to a Friend.

Heather is a great example of someone moving from Stranger to Friend virtually on her own. Through her own need, she discovered us and got to *know* us on our website. In this case, our search engine optimization work helped ensure Heather would at least know we existed. Now once Heather landed on our website, she immediately became our website's responsibility to quickly deepen both her knowledge and liking of Ugly Mug Marketing. That is part of the beauty of the Natural Progression. It gives us a lens through which we can evaluate all components of our marketing. In this case, when we understand the goal of our website is to increase *knowing* and *liking,* we can then design and build our website around those intentions. Spend a minute thinking through all your marketing tools and evaluate how they specifically help people transition through the Natural Progression.

As you can see from Heather's example, the Natural Progression is always at play. Following the Natural Progression

STRATEGIC MARKETING
is about holding
EACH DOLLAR
accountable for a
SPECIFIC RESULT.

#FULLCIRCLEMARKETING ⓘ

means you strategically think through each stage your pro-spective customers will pass through on their way to becom-ing Evangelists for you. Let's take a minute to quickly look at a proactive example of converting Strangers into Friends.

YOUR FIRST CAMPAIGN

KISS. Keep. It. Simple. Stupid. Don't worry, I'm not calling you stupid. It's a reminder to myself. Don't know if it's in my DNA, or due to my super-short attention span, but I'm noto-rious for making the simplest things complex. Following the Natural Progression ensures I keep it simple by following the natural flow. Let's do a quick walk-through of how simple it can be to set up your first campaign.

The first step, at least for people like me who love to complicate things, is to remember the only goal for your initial campaign is to move people from Strangers to Friends. Thanks to your customer avatar, you know who you need to reach. Knowing your "who" also provides direction as to where you need to run your first campaign. For example, if your customer avatar is 50—65 year old males who are C-level executives, that greatly shapes where you consider running your campaigns. Now that you know the *who* and *where* for your campaign, let's look at a scenario together.

Congratulations! You are now in charge of marketing for a coffee shop. Not just any coffee shop, but THE coffee shop in your town. This is an independent coffee shop with soul. The type of place you intentionally go out of your way for on your road trips. Let's start marketing!

Thanks to the diverse crowd your coffee shop attracts, there are several different avatars you could choose to reach with your marketing. For simplicity's sake, let's say the avatar we want to reach is coffee lovers who work within a one mile radius of your shop, and Facebook is the platform we want to use.

The first step is deciding how we can get these people to know about us. We don't need to over-engineer this step, but we must ensure our ad stands out in their crowded Facebook news-feed. A video of something our

The goal of your first campaign is to move people from Strangers to Friends. Nothing more!

target market would recognize will help cut through the clutter. So we walk one block down from our shop to the intersection where two busy streets meet, and record a short 15 second time lapse video of cars passing by. That video will become the creative we use for our ad.

To further draw people a bit deeper into the ad, we would add, "Recognize this intersection?", as text over the top portion of the video. Next, we'll draft the actual text that will appear along with our video. Here's a draft:

Do you recognize this intersection? We thought so! Did you know that when you cross this intersection you are less than one block away from the best coffee in town? See you soon!"

That's it. Nothing more. Again, your goal for this initial campaign is simply *knowing* and *liking*. Looking over the ad above you may be thinking, *I understand how this campaign would get people to know about our coffee shop, but how does it get people to "like" it?* Great question! Because when setting up the campaign inside Facebook, we would target people who live or work within a one mile radius of your coffee shop and are interested in coffee. The second part of our targeting is important. If we don't tell Facebook to show our ad to people who are interested in coffee, they will show our ad to everyone within a one mile radius, including those who hate coffee. And that would bring us back into the realm of ineffective and inefficient marketing, and neither you nor I want that!

Rest there. Resist the urge to do more. Resist the urge to offer a coupon or incentive to get people to come to your shop. For now, stay focused on *knowing* and *liking*.

As a marketer, your job is to look for ways to help move people from being Strangers to being Friends. Your marketing campaigns to Strangers simply need to focus on two elements: getting them to *know* you exist and demonstrating why they should *like* you. Don't over-complicate your campaigns directed towards Strangers. What do Strangers need to hear, see, and feel in order to *know* about you and begin *liking* you? Keep your campaigns centered around those answers, and you'll successfully move people from Strangers to Friends.

CHAPTER 6

WHY CAN'T WE BE FRIENDS

*H*aving a lot of friends is good, but having customers is infinitely better! Go too long without turning your Friends into Customers and it won't be long before you are out of business. As we talked about in the last chapter, the key distinction between a Stranger and a Friend is that a Friend *knows* and *likes* you. Without those two components, people will not continue through the Natural Progression and will never purchase your product or service. And having customers happens to be extremely important for your bank account.

In our effort to keep our marketing both efficient and effective, it's important to remember that not everyone will flow all the way through the Natural Progression. No need to sound the alarm or become discouraged. This is normal and natural.

Remember Heather from the previous chapter? Imagine after her initial web search for a website design company, Heather clicked the link and completely hated our website.

She hated the colors, the style, and the look and feel. What would she have done? Simple—she would have clicked or swiped back to her search results and clicked on another one of the search results. The problem for us would be that she didn't take the time to get to *know* a bit more about us. Here's the thing: there is nothing wrong with that. It would be foolish for us to get upset because she didn't hire us to build her new website. We understand that our services aren't right for everyone. At that point, Heather would no longer be in our Natural Progression, as she would have removed herself from the process.

Now let's switch back to the assumption that Heather liked what she saw on our site, and through more research starts believing that we might be able to design a remarkable website for her. What's likely to happen next? At some point, it may not be in the immediate future, she will take additional steps to ensure the initial trust she felt for us can be validated. This could mean reading more reviews, talking to some of our previous clients, scheduling a consultation with our team, or some combination of those. If those additional actions confirm her initial beliefs, chances are good she will hire us and become a Customer.

You see, the biggest factor in helping someone move from the Friend to Customer stage is trust. No one is going to hand over hard-earned money without trust in your company and your product or service. A key distinction is that this trust is multi-dimensional. For people to make a purchase, they have to trust:

- that the benefit they receive from your product/service is going to be of more value to them than the price they pay,

- that your product/service is going to do what it says it will do,
- that your company will deliver the product/service when you say you will
- that your company is going to stand behind (warranty) the product/service in the event something is defective or doesn't work.

Each of those are critical elements of the trust you must work to build. It's only once you've invested the time, energy, and effort to build trust that you can expect a Friend to become a Customer.

Many businesses can never scale because they aren't intentional about manufacturing trust into their marketing during the early stages of business growth. When businesses are first getting started, most often all of their initial customers are family and friends. That's a wonderful thing; at least it's wonderful until you run out of family and friends to sell to. You see, what most new business owners take for granted is the trust that is inherent with their family and friends. It doesn't take much trust building to sell your product to someone who already trusts you. But as you move farther and farther away from those who "know" you, the need for trust increases.

One way to think about it is degrees of separation. The more degrees that separate you from your prospective customer, the more time you will need to spend building trust to help them transition from Friend to Customer.

Here's what it looks like:

The lesson here is that if you're in the early stages of business growth, it's important to begin thinking through how you're going to incorporate trust elements into your marketing. Yes, it takes time. Yes, I know you already have a lot going on. But being intentional is being strategic. And being strategic is better than just hoping and praying.

YOUR TRUST CAMPAIGNS

Our goal for these campaigns is simple: build trust. Where trust goes, money flows. Learning to build trust though your marketing can feel a bit daunting, but it doesn't have to be. Thanks to trust being multi-dimensional, there are plenty of options for our campaigns. Keep in mind the entire goal of these campaigns is to move people from Friends to Customers, and nothing more.

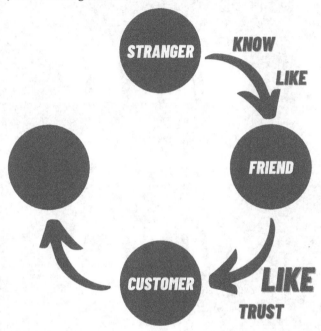

The first step is easy. All you need to do is select the type of trust your campaign is going to focus on building. Here's what I mean: Do you need to build trust around the value your product or service delivers? Do your Friends need a bit more trust that your product is going to do what they believe it should do? Or maybe you should focus on building trust that your company will stand behind your service when things don't go well. It's possible that a combination of all the above may be needed.

WHERE
trust goes,
MONEY
flows!

Every business is different, and therefore the type of trust needed when progressing from Friend to Customer can vary. If your company is new, but you sell a product that is similar to other competitors, then you may need to focus on building trust with your company. If you sell a high-ticket product or service, you may need to center these campaigns around trust that your products or services will produce the results your Friends desire.

At this point, you may start to feel a bit overwhelmed by the choices you have for your trust- building campaigns, and that's okay. It's okay to feel overwhelmed, but it's not okay to allow that feeling to stop you in your tracks. Remember, the first part of being strategic with your marketing is making decisions thoughtfully, and not just throwing stuff at the wall and hoping something sticks. So how do you know which trust campaign to start with? The easy way to make the decision is to trust your gut. Instinctively, you have a hunch as to which trust campaign is most needed to turn your Friends into Customers, so start with that one. Will it be the right one? You won't know until you try, which leads to the next part of strategic marketing.

Strategic marketing is about making thoughtful decisions, and then testing those decisions. And if you're feeling overwhelmed, keep this in mind. By selecting a particular trust-building campaign, you aren't committing to running that campaign forever. You are merely committing to testing your decision to see if it was correct. If your decision was correct, great! If not, make another decision and test it. Part of the beauty of the Natural Progression is that it gives you the ability to diagnose individual components of your marketing campaigns, allowing you to pinpoint the exact weak spots and quickly make adjustments.

TRUSTING YOUR COFFEE SHOP

Let's check in with your coffee shop. How are your *knowing* and *liking* campaigns going? Glad to hear they are going well! Now that you've successfully moved people from Strangers to Friends, let's start converting your Friends into Customers through trust campaigns. Your goal is simple: get your Friends to open their wallets and hand you money. Based on what you've learned so far, what type of trust campaign do you need to create? Let's explore this a bit more.

Since your coffee shop is located in what is predominantly a business district, one of the things you've learned is that most of your customers value speed. They want to be able to run over during a break to grab a beverage and a snack without having to wait in a long line. You've observed this by watching customers in business attire leave without ordering when the line is too long or moving too slow. Based on these observations, you decide to focus on building trust around speed—providing drinks and snacks quickly.

What can you say, do, or demonstrate to build trust regarding your shop's speed and efficiency? Several ideas come to mind, but here are a couple to consider. You could guarantee their drink within a certain amount of time. Remember the classic Dominos Pizza ads, "delivered in 30 minutes or less, or it's free!" Could you possibly make a similar guarantee?

If so, the creative for your campaign could be a great photo of one of your baristas handing a customer a drink with a caption saying, "Your Beverage, In Your Hand, In 5 Minutes or it's Free!" I'll be the first to admit, that campaign would be a bit risky, but if you can consistently pull it off, it would certainly build trust. Let's look at another trust-building campaign we could run.

One of the best ways to build trust is through social proof. Allowing your current customers to vouch for your speed and efficiency would be extremely effective. This social proof campaign could be centered around either a series of customer images or videos. The theme would be to highlight various customers talking about their favorite beverage and how they are able to get in and out quickly.

> *People would rather trust strangers they've never met, than trust you! Think about it. You wouldn't buy a new tube of toothpaste on Amazon without first scrolling down and looking at the reviews. In this instance, you are trusting absolute strangers over what the toothpaste company says in all their marketing messages. As marketers, we can't forget that people are naturally distrusting of what we say, because they know we are biased. Therein lies the power of social proof.*

What other trust-based campaigns could you run to convert Friends into Customers for your coffee shop? Take a minute to think of a few. It's a great mental exercise that will help strengthen your marketing muscles. Between the examples I provided above, and the campaigns you thought of, which will you use to build trust? Now, with that campaign in mind, let's briefly talk about where to target that campaign.

Thanks to the simple flow of the Natural Progression, we don't have to waste our time figuring out who to target. We know this message will be directed at the Friends we created through our previous (*knowing* and *liking*) campaign(s). Where you'll run your trusting campaigns is determined simply by putting the ads where your Friends are now congregated. Here are a couple of examples. If you used Facebook videos to move people from Strangers to Friends, you could create a custom audience based on who watched your *liking* and *knowing* video campaign. On the other hand, if your campaign encouraged Strangers to sign up for your newsletter, you could send your trust campaign directly to them.

Don't over-analyze; don't overthink. Keep your focus on merely moving Friends to Customers by building trust. Depending on the product or service you sell, it may be necessary to have several trust campaigns (one for each of the dimensions we discussed on page XX) running. But don't allow this to overwhelm you. Start by creating one *trust* campaign that covers one of the dimensions you need to cover. Once that one is up and running successfully, move to the next. One. Step. At. A. Time. You've got this!

Note: Before we move on, it's important to know that you may be able to keep your *knowing, liking,* and *trusting* campaigns running all the time as evergreen campaigns. This will be determined based on your specific goals and objectives.

If you've been strategic in their creation and tested them, they will help continually push people through the Natural Progression.

CHAPTER 7

PUTTING MONEY IN THE BANK

*F*ar too many entrepreneurs and marketers mistakenly believe getting people to the Customer stage is the ultimate goal of business. Getting people to pull out their wallets and give you money in exchange for your product or service is certainly worthy of celebration, but wise marketers understand this is merely the beginning of an entirely new, and far more important, process. We'll go through this new process in more detail in the next chapter, but for now we want to be sure your product or service doesn't violate the trust you carefully built during the previous stage.

The quickest way to violate trust is by failing to meet expectations. The challenge in meeting expectations is that every customer is entitled to have their own set of expectations. Dealing with a wide range of expectations can be frustrating, but only if we don't embrace them as beautiful things. This requires a mindset shift.

Often we spend far too much time and energy complaining about our customers' ever changing expectations. We instead need to shift our focus to dealing with reality, and stop trying to change it. The reality is that customer expectations are in a constant state of change. Over time, their expectations seem to continually get more and more complex and difficult. That's reality. Don't waste your time fighting it. Embrace it.

Let's look at what one of the most successful entrepreneurs of all time, Jeff Bezos, Amazon Founder, has to say about it.

> One thing I LOVE about customers is that they are divinely discontent.

Notice, he doesn't just tolerate the fact that customers are *"divinely discontent."* He LOVES it. Jeff continues...

> Their expectations are never static—they go up. It's human nature. People have a voracious appetite for a better way, and yesterday's 'wow' quickly becomes today's 'ordinary.'

> ...I sense that the same customer empowerment phenomenon is happening broadly across everything we do at Amazon and most other industries as well. You cannot rest on your laurels in this world. Customers won't have it.

Notice, he doesn't complain about unrealistic customer expectations. He knows it won't do any good. He knows Amazon MUST keep improving and innovating, along with empowering their customers. I don't know about you, but

Effective marketers train themselves to think long-term.

I've certainly been guilty of complaining about customers' never-ending demands and their continuously evolving expectations. And what good have those complaints done to me? Nada!

Instead of complaining, what if I —what if you—invested that time and energy into finding ways to exceed our customers' ever-evolving expectations? I have no empirical evidence, but I'd be willing to bet we'd both be better off.

Accept the fact that customers are going to constantly expect more, and often for less money. Take time to investigate how you can start empowering your customers—empowering them to solve their problems and to share their experience with others. But before we get too far ahead of ourselves, let's spend a few minutes talking through our options once we convert our Friends into Customers.

YOUR OPTIONS AS A MARKETER

As marketers, we, rightfully so, have the reputation for being short-sighted. Part of this is due to our fundamental misunderstanding of marketing, and the other part is due to imaginary lines we draw. If we allow our misunderstanding or imaginary lines to stop us from continuing our work, we sell ourselves short. You see, if we keep working a bit more, we'll have the ability to turn ordinary Customers into Evangelists. In the next chapter, we will walk through the specific steps you will need to take, but for now let's focus on ensuring you have the right mindset.

To become an effective marketer, you have to train yourself to think long-term and to see the big picture. If we aren't careful we get hung up focusing on the individual pieces and components of our marketing system. Great marketers are able to step back and metaphorically look down on their marketing and see the entire system. They can see how each campaign builds on the next, quickly spotting weaknesses and friction points within the system they've created. Having this big picture view also enables great marketers to see customers as a point of leverage for their marketing system.

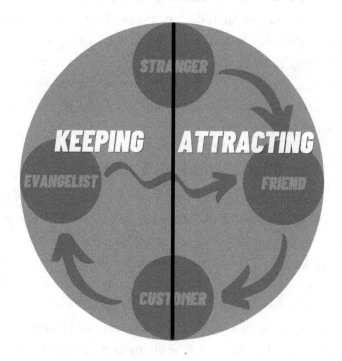

Marketing magic begins when you are able to turn ordinary Customers into Evangelists for your products. Creating Evangelists doesn't start with our customers; it starts with our mindset and what we believe marketing is. The first place to start is ensuring we have the proper definition of marketing. Remember, marketing is your ability to both *attract* and *keep* a customer. For most marketers their mindset is limited to the *attracting* side. It's as if there's an imaginary line down the middle of the Natural Progression. Everything on the right (the attracting side) is our responsibility, and everything on the left (the keeping side) is somebody else's job.

Here's the thing; these lines aren't your fault. Most of the time we begin drawing these imaginary lines as a result of job titles. We create fictional boundaries around where our work begins and ends. For many of us, we need to retrain our thinking. We need to erase the supposed line down the middle of the Natural Progression. We need to give intentional thought to how our products are packaged, if they arrive on time, and if our product delivers value and exceeds expectations.

So I challenge you to shift your mindset—to step back and view your marketing in its entirety, as a whole system. Think of getting Customers as the first half of your job and learning to transform your Customers into Evangelists as the second half. By embracing the entire Natural Progression, you will begin building an army of loyal Customers to help spread your message—an army of Evangelists.

PART III

THE FULL CIRCLE

CHAPTER 8

EVANGELIZING THE WORLD

"*E*vangelist" is a bit of a strange word to find in a marketing book. When you think of evangelists, what comes to mind? Not sure about you, but for most people the term evangelists has a religious connotation, and rightly so. But at its core, evangelist means *"a person who seeks to convert others."* As a marketer, what more could you possibly want than passionate customers telling others about your amazing products or services?

Evangelists are people who go out and share your message with the world. It sounds simple, and it can be, but if you want to build an army of Evangelists, it requires an intentional effort on your part. Your effort for turning ordinary Customers into Evangelists should begin with these three critical components. Make sure your Customers:

- are thrilled (aka, you've clearly exceeded their expectations) with the product or service you have delivered.

- know what to tell others about you.
- have the tools and resources to share you with others.

Take a look at the Natural Progression graphic below, and you'll discover the power of creating Evangelists is that you completely bypass the prospect stage. This is the exact same process that happens when you generate referrals. If you're like most entrepreneurs, then you already know both the power and importance of referrals for your business. But what you may not have realized, at least until now, is that there are specific steps you can take to help ensure a constant flow of referrals. By understanding and working with the

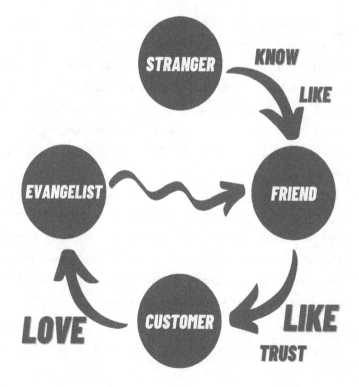

Natural Progression, you can begin building a steady stream of referrals flowing into your company.

So where do we start? First we must clarify our customers' actual expectations. Once we clearly understand their expectations, we can begin putting systems and processes in place to ensure we consistently exceed their expectations. But creating an army of Evangelists doesn't happen by merely surpassing expectations. After we've exceeded their expectations, we have to give them the language we'd like for them to use when sharing with others. Giving them language not only makes it easier for them to share with others, but it also helps ensure they communicate the right message. Now that we've exceeded their expectations and given them language, the final step is providing them with tools. Let's explore each of these steps in more detail.

1. EXCEED EXPECTATIONS

Research conducted by Bain & Company found that **80% of companies believe they are delivering a superior service.** And yet, **only 8% of customers believe that they are receiving superior service.** Let that sink in for a minute. If this data is true, which I believe it is, this means the majority of businesses out there believe the service they provide to their customers is better than it is in reality.

All of my years of working with entrepreneurs confirms Bain & Company's findings. We, as entrepreneurs, are often a bit delusional when it comes to the level of service we're providing. There are likely many reasons for our unrealistic beliefs but none of them matter. What matters is accepting reality—accepting the fact that just because we believe something to be true doesn't make it true. So if we can't trust our own thoughts about the level of service we're providing, what should we do? There are several ways to find the *truth* about your level of service, but here are three specific tactics:

A. ASK

The first approach is simply asking your customers. After all, if you want to know if you are indeed exceeding expectations, who better to ask?

Although it's a straightforward approach, that doesn't mean it's easy to uncover the truth. One of the biggest challenges with getting customers to reveal the truth is that they don't want to hurt your feelings. If you want to get beyond the surface level responses and get to the heart of how they're really feeling, you'll want to either ensure their feedback is completely anonymous, or have a third-party complete the surveying for you. Both of these approaches make it a little safer for customers to share their honest feedback and feelings.

B. BELOW. EXPECTED. ABOVE.

Another way to find the truth about expectations is to chart out what would be considered below, at, and above expectations, and use these findings as a litmus test against the level of service you are currently providing. Here's how to go about this process:

Take out a sheet of paper and at the top in the center write, "What IS expected." Now, down the middle of the page, under this heading, write out everything that a reasonable person has the right to expect when purchasing your product or service. You'll want to answer questions like:

- How long do they expect to have to wait?
- How much do they expect to pay?
- How easy do they expect it to be to use your product/service?
- What do they expect to happen in the event there's an issue?
- What do they expect the post-sale follow up will be?

Once you've identified and written out all your customers' expectations, it's now time to go back through each question and discover what would have to be true to not reach their expectations. For example, if they expect to receive your product/service within 48 hours, on the left side (under the Less Than Expected section) you would write, "longer than 48 hours." After completing the Less Than Expected Section, it's now time to move to the next part of the process.

On the right side of your page you're going to write the words, "EXCEEDS EXPECTATIONS." Under this section you'll go through each question and ask yourself, "What would it take to clearly exceed expectations in this area?" For example, if they expect to receive your product or service within 48 hours, it would clearly exceed their expectations if it was delivered within 24 hours. Now complete this process for each area where a customer could possibly have an expectation.

Take some time now to complete this exercise. Once completed, come back and we'll talk about the final step.

C.THE LITMUS TEST

At this point, you should have one page that clearly identifies what exceeding your customers' expectations would look like. But merely having this piece of paper is of little value. The value comes from using it as a litmus test against real transactions. Randomly pick a few recent transactions and honestly evaluate each of the areas of expectations. Mark whether you fell short, met, or exceeded expectations.

It's important to remember that the goal of this exercise isn't to make you feel good about your business. The goal is to help ensure you're in the position to create Evangelists for your business, and the only way to reach that goal is to seek the truth. Discovering the truth will help ensure you consistently exceed expectations. Once you're consistently exceeding expectations, it's time to move to the next step in the process and give them language.

2. GIVE THEM LANGUAGE

In today's world, having customers eager and willing to share with others is a monumental accomplishment, but what if they don't spread the right message? Their experience with us and our product or service may have been wonderful, but that doesn't mean they know how to tell others about their experience. Part of our job of creating Evangelists is ensuring they know the right *language* (the words that will have the most impact) when they share with others.

The words people use to describe our company, or our products, determine what others think about it. Boiled down to its core, your brand is what others think about you, not what you think about yourself. As we discussed earlier, you may believe you provide amazing service, but what you believe doesn't matter if it isn't the truth. And what others believe to be true about your company or your products determines the language they use when describing your company and products to their family and friends.

The question becomes—if our brand is about what others think and say about us, then how do we go about sculpting what they say about us? How do we influence the language they use?

USE DESCRIPTIVE LANGUAGE

Descriptive language helps people *see* what you're saying. Here's an example.

Speak in benefits, not features.

An animal that lives in the water.

A fish.

A piranha.

As the language moves from vague to specific, what people see in their minds becomes more clear. Descriptive language evokes emotion. Emotion leads to action. And action is what we're after.

Your language needs to center around knowing, liking, and building trust.

We think in features. Customers focus on benefits. Our language must clearly articulate the benefits, the end results our customers are after. We've all heard the old marketing adage—no one wants a drill; everyone wants the hole. As cliche as it is, it's true.

One of the simplest ways to ensure your language is benefits-focused is to ask yourself, "which means?" For example, *our websites load 98% faster than websites built on Word-Press, which means more of your website visitors will stay on your website.*

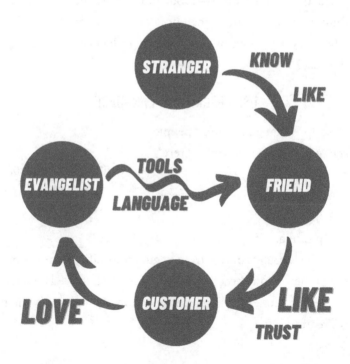

YOUR BRAND
is what others
THINK ABOUT YOU,
not what you think
ABOUT YOURSELF.

As you can see, by adding "which means," you get closer to the benefit. But you don't have to stop after asking "which means" once, you need to keep asking. Using the same example from above, let's keep asking "which means."

Our websites load 98% faster than websites built on Word-Press, which means more of your website visitors will stay on your website. Which means you'll have a lower bounce rate on your website. Which means your website will have a higher conversion rate. Which means your visitor-to-sale ratio will automatically improve.

So if we were to take that to client-specific language, it may look like this: *Do you want a website that automatically generates leads and produces sales? If so, you need to call my friends at Ugly Mug Marketing.*

Don't get sloppy with your language. Help sculpt and shape it.

3. GIVE THEM TOOLS

If we want our Evangelists to share, we have to make it easy. We have to give them tools. A tool for Evangelists is anything that makes it easy for them to share with others. This can be anything from a business card, to a social media graphic, to an extra goodie they can share with their family or friends. The tool you provide your Evangelist should also help indoctrinate the friend or family member with whom they share. It should help them know more about you, like what your company, product, or service could do for them, and begin building trust.

Here are a few ideas to help get your creative juices flowing.

- After someone completes a purchase on your website, offer them a discount for sharing on their social media.
- In your confirmation email (post-order), provide them with a discount to share with their friends and family.
- If you ship a physical product, include something extra they will want to share with others.
- Celebrate anniversaries (1 month post-purchase, 1 year post-purchase) with an incentive to get them to share with others.

Yes, there are a lot of options. Don't overthink it. Don't overcomplicate it. Choose one thing and start working on implementing it into your post-purchase process. You already know this, but it's worth repeating here... if you attempt to start or implement too many things at one time, you'll likely end up not finishing any of them. I'd recommend setting the goal of implementing one new tool for your Evangelists each quarter. For some of you, that may feel a bit slow, but at the end of the year you will have four new tools for your Evangelists to use.

Evangelists don't have to be customers. Sometimes your best Evangelist may have never been a customer. Look for others who serve the same customer avatar as you, and begin a relationship with them. Let's look at a quick example of this.

Let's assume you own a gym. The first step is to simply think through all the other places (businesses, organizations, etc.) where your potential customers may hang out. Here are a few questions to think through:

- Where do they get their groceries?
- Where do they eat out?
- Where do they shop for their athletic gear?
- Where do they buy their recreational equipment (bicycles, kayaks, etc.)?
- Where do they go to participate in their hobbies (golf courses, walking trails, etc.)?

With this list in hand, it's time to begin looking for creative ways you could establish referral relationships with these places. The more of these relationships you establish, the better. Each of these relationships has the potential to become an evergreen source and flow of referrals back into your business. To help get your creative juices flowing, let's look at a sample scenario together.

As a gym owner, you know that, other than exercise, the next biggest factor in maintaining good health is nutrition. So you approach the owners of a couple of restaurants in your area that are known for serving healthier food options, and ask them if they would be interested in a referral relationship. They would offer some form of discount for your gym members in exchange for you promoting their restaurant inside your gym. They would also agree to allow you to place an exclusive 60-day free trial coupon at their check-out counter.

The beauty of these types of relationships is they are mutually beneficial, and they leverage each other's most powerful asset, the existing customer base. Before moving on to the next chapter, work through the three steps for turning Customers into Evangelists, and spend a few minutes creating a list of potential non-customer relationships that you can establish.

THE INTERMISSION

How's it going? Are you still with me? I hope what we've talked about so far is making sense, and a few new lightbulbs are going off for you. Before we move on and talk through how to ensure people flow smoothly through your Natural Progression, I want to take just a minute to do a recap on how to convert Customers into Evangelists. Mastering this transition enables you to build the marketing equivalent of a perpetual motion machine, with a never-ending source of new Friends flowing into your business. So here are the five steps you need to take:

STEP 1

The first step in the process of turning Customers into Evangelists is to have a clear understanding of your current process for fulfilling customer orders. write down everything that happens from the moment someone becomes a Customer. Take a sheet of paper and go ahead and list out every single interaction that takes place after someone purchases from you.

STEP 2

Now it's time to create a list of what is industry norm, or what your customers expect after a purchase. For example, if you sell shoes online, first your customers assume they will receive an order receipt email with shipping information. Next, they receive a notification when the package is shipped. And finally, they receive their shoes via UPS. So, those three steps are considered industry norms, and it is what customers purchasing your type of product expect.

STEP 3

Now go back through your list (from Step 1) and ask, "What could we do differently from what we currently do that would be remarkable to our customers?"

Using the shoe example from above, what if you decided to not only send an order confirmation email, but then when the package ships to send them a photo of their shoes being put into the package? What if in every package you inserted an extra pair of shoestrings? What if ten days after they receive the shoes, someone from your customer service department called them to see how the shoes fit?

Go ahead and list a few ways you can exceed your customers' expectations and determine how you can insert these into your fulfillment process. They don't have to be big or expensive—just simple ways you can get your customer to say "wow."

STEP 4

In Step 3 you figured out specific things you can do to impress your customers enough for them to want to tell others about you. Now in this step, we need to figure out specifically how we can get our customers to share with others. Create a list of all the various ways that your customers can share your message with others. Here a few examples:

- On your order thank you page, ask them to share their purchase in exchange for a discount off their next order.
- If you sell a lost-cost item, include an extra one with their order, and have a message saying, "We've included an extra X as our way of thanking you for being

an awesome customer! We hope you'll share it with a friend who also loves X."

- If your product goes into an office environment, include something extra that is cool enough for them to want to display it on their desk.
- Create social media graphics they can quickly and easily share on their channels.
- Have an ongoing contest that rewards people for sharing photos of them using your product on their social media pages.

STEP 5

Go back through the list you created in Step 4 and select the easiest one to launch. Set a goal to have the method you selected launched within the next four weeks. Now break your plan into four micro goals, one goal for each of the next four weeks. For example, if you decided to create a share feature on your after-order thank you page, what would be the four micro-goals you would need to set? Maybe they are:

1. Talk with ten customers to determine what would incentivize them the most to share on social media.
2. Determine what coding or third-party application you will utilize to make the share feature functional.
3. Create the graphics and launch the share feature on a test page.
4. Test, adjust, and implement.

By taking the time to follow and implement the steps above, you are immediately beginning to differentiate your business from your competitors. That should get you excited! You are being strategic, not only about attracting new customers, but also in turning them into Evangelists for your company.

I don't know about you, but I can feel it. There's momentum starting to build around your marketing system. But we're not quite finished. We have a bit more work to do together.

CHAPTER 9

DON'T BE STUPID

There are certain things *they* say you should never talk about. Politics and religion are two that come to mind. Then there are certain things you, as a marketer, *should* talk about. Keeping the path clear and obstacle-free for your prospective customers is one of them. But just because we should do something doesn't always translate into actually doing what we should. It never ceases to amaze me how we as marketers often create obstacles to our success. We invest time, energy and effort getting people to know, like, and trust us, only to destroy it all with one stupid decision.

Imagine the path of taking someone from Stranger to Friend, and then from a Friend to Customer as a road. Your job is to ensure the road is debris- and obstacle-free. You also have to remove your competitors' signs that may tempt your prospects to leave your road and start down your competitor's road. Both jobs are important (keeping the road free of debris and obstacles and removing your competitors signs), but we have infinitely more control over keeping the debris and obstacles off our road. But if we aren't careful, we'll end up wasting precious time focused on what our competitors are doing instead of removing the debris and obstacles from our own road.

Debris are small, ugly, unexpected things on your road that cause prospective customers to briefly pause and step over them. The danger with debris isn't in its size, as most of it can easily be stepped over. The danger with debris is that each piece is unexpected, unpleasant, and erodes trust.

Obstacles, on the other hand, are anything on your road that requires extra steps on your prospective customers' journey down your road. Obstacles are more likely to end someone's journey down your road, because obstacles are not easy to step over. Potential clients are forced to either climb over them or forge a path around them. Anything that makes it more difficult to purchase your product or service decreases the likelihood of a sale.

Over time, debris and obstacles can appear on our road as a natural byproduct of growth. This is normal and to be expected. The fact that debris and obstacles appear isn't the problem. The problem is we are often oblivious to them. The things we don't see, can—and often do—hurt our businesses. Here's an important lesson: Just because you don't see something, doesn't mean it doesn't exist. The best way to ensure you see the debris and obstacles is to see the road through someone else's windshield—specifically through your customers' and prospective customers' windshields.

Their opinion of your road is more important than your own beliefs about how beautiful your road may be.

The danger of debris on your road is that it trips prospective customers up and slows their journey to becoming a Customer. There are few things more frustrating for a marketer than to create a high-converting lead-generation campaign, only to then lose these potential customers due to debris on the road. Here are a few examples of obstacles and debris:

- Not accepting American Express is debris or an obstacle
- Not being open when your Customer is ready to make a purchase is an obstacle
- Not having a real person answer your phone is another form of debris
- Trash in your parking lot is debris (in this case both figurative and literal)
- Taking days to respond to emails or messages is debris
- Charging extra for "handling" is debris
- Not having a product in stock is an obstacle
- Broken links on your website are debris
- A dirty entrance door is debris

Alone, none of the above may prevent a prospective customer from purchasing. But allow a couple of pieces of debris to remain on your road, and you will certainly start having prospects leave your road. And when people leave your road, it directly affects your conversion ratios. So, as a marketer, it's important for you to spend time looking for and removing debris and obstacles. Here are a few scenarios to think through:

IF YOUR CALL TO ACTION IS FOR PEOPLE TO CALL, HERE ARE FEW THINGS TO CONTEMPLATE:

- What if they call before or after hours? What impression will they have?
- How do we sound when we answer the phone?
- How are phone messages taken? How are they responded to?
- Does the person answering the phone expect their call?
- Does the person answering the phone have the answers?
- How many times does your phone ring before it's answered?

IF YOUR CALL TO ACTION IS FOR PEOPLE TO VISIT YOUR WEBSITE, HERE ARE A FEW THINGS TO CONSIDER:

- Do they arrive on a page that makes sense for them? Is the page in line with their interests and desires?
- Does the page style match your offer?
- Does the page load fast?
- Is the next action you need them to take abundantly clear to them?
- If they have further questions, is it clear exactly how they can get answers?

IF YOUR CALL TO ACTION IS FOR PEOPLE TO VISIT YOUR STORE, HERE ARE A FEW THINGS TO EVALUATE:

- Does the outside of your building match the brand you want to portray?

- Is there anything leading up to your entrance that could possibly send the wrong message?
- Once they enter, can they quickly find where your call to action was leading?
- Does your team know to expect these prospective customers?
- Does your team know how to answer their questions and concerns?

Once we've invested all the time, energy, and effort getting someone to take action, we don't want to blow it by making things difficult or frustrating. Our job as marketers isn't merely coming up with creative campaigns. Our job is ensuring the entire buying process is smooth and seamless.

When it comes to getting people to move quickly and smoothly through the process of Stranger to Friend to Customer, the very first step is to ensure all debris and obstacles are removed. This isn't a one time event; it requires constant and continual effort. You should expect to constantly have to remove obstacles and debris. It's no different than cleaning your house. You don't clean your house and expect it to stay clean forever, particularly if you have kids. Business growth brings complexity, and complexity is a breeding ground for obstacles and debris.

A regular "cleaning schedule" is the simplest solution to ensuring your road stays clear. And once you believe you've cleared all the debris and obstacles, you'll want to have an outsider evaluate the condition of your road. Just as no parent wants to believe they have an ugly baby, no entrepreneur

EFFECTIVE MARKETING doesn't happen **BY ACCIDENT.**

#FULLCIRCLEMARKETING

EFFECTIVE MARKETING happens when **INTENTION AND ACTION** collide.

wants to believe they have a cluttered road. It's worth mentioning again that our opinion of the condition of our road doesn't matter. The only opinion that matters is the opinion of those we hope will traverse down our road. Be sure you invest the time, energy and effort getting objective opinions.

GREASING THE ROAD

Once your road is clear, the next step is to look for ways to make your road slick. Your goal should be to make it so that as soon as people step on your road, they slide effortlessly to the point of pulling out their wallet and handing you money. This requires intent. It requires continual attention. If you aren't intentional in your efforts, chances are good your competitors will be. In fact, let me rephrase that. Your competitors are most likely going to be intentional whether you are or not. That makes it all the more important for you to be deliberate, don't you think? Don't overcomplicate this. Simply get in the habit of asking, "What can we do to make it easier and more convenient for people to do business with us instead of our competitors?" and then implement based on your answers.

Be careful not to base your decisions on what your competitors are doing, what others in your industry are doing, and certainly not on what's most convenient for you. Your decisions should be guided by one thing—what's best for your customers and prospective customers.

Today, Amazon is the obvious king of ecommerce. But not that long ago, this wasn't the case. Long before they ruled the online world, they obsessed over removing obstacles and debris, and greasing the road for their potential customers. Here are few ways Amazon has worked to grease their road:

> **What can you do to make it easier for people to pull out their wallets and hand you money?**

- One-click purchasing
- Two-day shipping
- Same-day delivery
- Quick and painless returns
- Amazon Prime

This list doesn't seem impressive today, but it is when you consider that none of those things existed in the ecommerce space before Amazon launched them. And all the items on that list serve the purpose of making it easier and more convenient for people to purchase from Amazon.

What about you? What can you do to make it easier for people to pull out their wallets and hand you money? What would make doing business with you the obvious choice? I get it; spending time answering these questions may not feel like marketing. But it's important to remember that the highest-converting marketing campaign in the world can be quickly sabotaged by debris and obstacles on your prospective customer's path. Spend time today cleaning up your road and making it easier for people to hand you money. Do those two things well, and all of your marketing gets a bit easier.

CHAPTER 10

STOP BEING SO DEMANDING

Stop demanding so much from your marketing campaigns. Maybe you're different, but most marketers demand too much from each of their marketing campaigns. They hold each campaign to unrealistic expectations. These unwarranted expectations are a natural byproduct of taking a tactical approach (instead of a strategic) to your marketing. When you are constantly chasing the *latest and greatest* tactic, the bulk of your time gets wasted in the pursuit of finding the next big thing. If you aren't careful, you'll spend so much time trying to discover the latest marketing hack that you don't have much time or energy left for launching your actual campaigns. And when you don't leave enough time to strategically think through your campaign development, you are forced to rely on the Prayer Strategy.

You may not be familiar with the Prayer Strategy, but I'd be willing to bet you've used it. The Prayer Strategy works like this: once you finally get around to developing and launching your campaign, you don't have much time or energy left, so you launch it and then pray it works. Look, I'm not against prayer, but don't you think you should have a better strategy in place for marketing your organization?

When we choose to be strategic with our marketing, it forces us to have realistic expectations. The flow of the Natural Progression helps keep our expectations in check and gives us a lens through which to view each specific marketing campaign in our strategy. Without this unique lens, we often fall prey to demanding far too much from each campaign. We mistakenly believe, whether consciously or not, that one campaign is capable of instantaneously converting a Stranger into a Customer. Our optimism, coupled with our lack of time, causes us to lose sight of the natural way everyone makes buying decisions. When we forget the simple process of first getting people to know us, like us, and then trust us, we set ourselves up for both frustration and ineffective marketing.

STRUCTURING YOUR CAMPAIGNS

When you follow the Natural Progression, it provides you with a clear framework for how to structure your campaigns. No more guessing what type of campaigns you need to run or what your ads should say. With the Natural Progression as your guide, you now know you need at least three specific marketing campaigns: one to turn Strangers into Friends, another to turn Friends into Customers, and finally at least one campaign to turn Customers into Evangelists. The beauty is in the fact that guesswork is removed from your marketing by asking the following questions:

1. What campaign(s) am I running to get Strangers to know about our product, service, or company?
2. What campaign(s) am I running to get Strangers to "like" our product, service, or company?
3. What campaign(s) am I running to get Friends to trust that our product, service, or company will deliver exceptional value?
4. What campaign(s) am I running to turn Customers into Evangelists?

Do you see how the answers to these four foundational questions can become the center of your marketing campaigns? Learning to think about your marketing linearly, the same way people naturally make purchasing decisions, prevents you from becoming overwhelmed and demanding too much from any one of your marketing campaigns.

Our natural tendency is to launch a campaign and expect that it will somehow almost instantaneously cause people to pull out their wallets and hand over their money. And then when this doesn't happen, we begin to play the blame game. We blame the particular platform or medium we were running the campaign on, the tactic we were attempting to use, or even the guru whose advice we were attempting to follow. We scatter the blame around to everything and everyone. Occasionally, we even start blaming ourselves. We start thinking things like: I'm just not cut out for marketing, or I am terrible at creating ads that work. Playing the blame game is a losing game. You see, the blame game renders us powerless. It strips away the most powerful element in marketing, and that is the ability to own our failures.

Until we own our failures, we can't learn from them. When we blame our marketing failures on platforms, tactics, or gurus, we remove our ability to learn and grow. When it is the platform's fault, we waste time searching for the newest platform. When it's the tactic's fault, we grab at the tactic that all the marketing gurus are talking about. And when the marketing guru's strategy fails us, we look for the new guru who has discovered the latest tactic that is *killing it* on the hot new platform. In the midst of all this searching and discovering, we fail to look at the one person who is truly to blame, the person in the mirror.

Until we step off the hamster wheel of chasing the *latest and greatest*, we'll continue running hard while going nowhere. So as we begin to draw our time together to an end, I would like to encourage you to step off the hamster wheel and step into the Natural Progression. By using the Natural Progression as your guide, you can quickly and easily diagnose where your root marketing problem lies and make the needed adjustments without discarding your entire marketing strategy. Not creating enough Friends? Fix your Stranger to Friends Campaigns. Not converting enough Friends into Customers? No need to discard all of your marketing; just make adjustments to those specific campaigns.

Part of the beauty of following the Natural Progression is the ability to identify and adjust the exact campaign(s) that is not performing well. The other beautiful part is that following the Natural Progression removes most of the confusion and complexity that surrounds marketing.

My challenge for you is to stop violating the fundamental marketing laws (the Natural Progression and AIDA). With any law that you violate there are consequences, and the same is true when you disregard the Natural Progression or AIDA. Defy either of these and your consequence will be complicated, ineffective, and expensive marketing. It's only once you embrace the natural laws of marketing and use them to your advantage that you have a chance for both efficient and effective marketing campaigns.

Not that you need it, but in case you do, you have my permission to stop demanding so much from your marketing campaigns.

BRINGING IT ALL TOGETHER

*L*et's end where we began: marketing shouldn't be expensive, complex, or ineffective. At its core, marketing is nothing more than attracting and keeping customers. It's how you and your team go about accomplishing those two objectives that makes all the difference. One approach is to do as many marketing *things* as possible and pray for the best. The other is to step back and develop a marketing strategy that is in alignment with basic human psychology. Based on our conversation over the previous pages, I'm sure you know which approach I would recommend. But just because I recommend it, or even if you wholeheartedly agree with it, doesn't mean you'll do it. Taking action is hard. Breaking bad marketing habits is even harder.

Taking the strategic path with your marketing often makes you feel like you are on the slow path. While you are busy developing campaigns that follow the flow of the Natural Progression, your competitors have already made forty-seven posts and launched three Facebook campaigns. And if you are not careful, seeing their flurry of activity can tempt you to leave your important strategic work and join them in the chase for the latest tactic or guru. Don't give in to this temptation! Being strategic may feel like more work initially, and it may very well be. Your initial efforts, however, will be rewarded in the long run.

Let me close our time together with a question: are you carrying buckets, or are you building pipelines? Here's what I mean:

The small village had a big problem. Their only source of water, a well that had been dug more than thirty years ago, ran dry. Due to their hot, dry climate, the villagers couldn't survive more than a couple of days without a new source of water. The leaders of the village chose two of their most successful farmers to solve the water problem.

The first farmer quickly took several of his laborers from his fields, provided them buckets, and instructed them to begin the two-hour journey to the nearest fresh water stream and carry the water back. After four hours they returned with six buckets of water, to the cheers and celebration of their fellow villagers. Their celebration was short-lived, as six buckets of water wasn't enough for the entire village, so they immediately began their journey back to the stream. This journey became their existence.

Meanwhile, the second farmer seemed to have disappeared. The people in the village began to wonder what happened to her. The leaders of the village sent out a search party to discover what happened to her. After all, she had promised them fresh drinking water.

What they discovered was that instead of constantly running back and forth carrying buckets, the second farmer decided to take a more strategic approach. You see, she wasn't interested in solving the problem for a day, but in solving the problem indefinitely. When the search party found her, she and her laborers were in the process of constructing a waterline from the freshwater stream back towards the village. After two months, her waterline was completed. Now the village had access to fresh, cool water twenty-four hours a day, seven days a week.

The question I have for you is: Do you want to continue carrying buckets, or are you ready to build your waterline?

You may have to keep carrying buckets for a bit longer as you're building your waterline. That's completely fine. But now that you know how to build your own marketing waterline, it's not okay to keep carrying buckets indefinitely. Start planning your waterline right now.

Effective marketing doesn't happen by accident. Effective marketing happens when intention and action collide. I hope you will take what you've learned and begin implementing it, because you haven't really learned anything until you've applied it.

HOW TO APPLY THESE IDEAS TO YOUR BUSINESS

Over the years, I've helped thousands of entrepreneurs from around the world put an end to their marketing chaos and confusion and start getting results. I've compiled many of the most practical strategies and tools into a short bonus chapter. I think you'll find it to be an incredibly useful addition to the main ideas in *Full Circle Marketing*.

You can download this chapter at:
yourfullcirclebook.com/bonus

ABOUT THE AUTHOR

WAYNE MULLINS is a husband, father of 4, founder, CEO, entrepreneur and author. He's a generous soul; a risk taker; and an out-of-the-box, against-the-grain thinker & leader.

Over the past 20 years, Wayne Mullins has scaled multiple companies and helped hundreds of entrepreneurs do the same with their companies.

Ugly Mug Marketing has won the praises of some of the leading influencers in the business world such as Neil Patel (Founder of QuickSprout + Kissmetrics) and Chris Voss (Author of *Never Split the Difference*).

CONNECT WITH WAYNE ONLINE!

@fireyourself

@uglymugmarketing

To learn more, visit:

YourFullCircleMarketing.com

DID YOU ENJOY THIS BOOK?
CONSIDER SHARING IT WITH OTHERS

1 Share or mention the book on your social media using #fullcirclemarketing and tag @fireyourself

2 Write a book review on any book review site.

3 Send a copy to your friends or colleagues who you think would enjoy and be challenged by the content.

CPSIA information can be obtained
at www.ICGtesting.com
Printed in the USA
LVHW080129191121
703659LV00004B/8/J

9 780578 976518